HOW MANY IS ONE

POEMS BY JOANNA HAWTHORNE

Joanna Hawthorne

Copyright © 2005 by Joanna Hawthorne.

ISBN: Softcover   1-59926-868-X

All rights reserved. No part of this book may be reproduced or transmitted in any form or by any means, electronic or mechanical, including photocopying, recording, or by any information storage and retrieval system, without permission in writing from the copyright owner.

This book was printed in the United States of America.

To order additional copies of this book, contact:
Xlibris Corporation
1-888-795-4274
www.Xlibris.com
Orders@Xlibris.com
30133

CONTENTS

Dedication iii
Foreword v
Introduction vii

Part 1. ME ....
        Thoughts on Reaching Seventy 7
        My Stuff 9
        Summer Times 1939-1941 11
        Pemaquid 13
        Steps of Remembrance 17
        Freedom March 19

Part 2. WE ....
        He Said! She Said! 25
        The Quest 27
        Narcissus Revisited 29
        Resolution 31
        Using the Power 33
        Almost 35

Part 3. S/HE . . . .
- First Song 41
- Look At It! 43
- Somebody Goofed! 45
- Kritters 47
- The Grand Tour 49
- How Many Is One? 51

DEDICATION

I dedicate this book to Nectar,
Who pushed until I delivered.
A poem is truly a birth process,
And she never lost faith in my ability
To bring forth my very best.
With gratitude, thanks and love.

FOREWORD

"I don't sound old, just wise." With these lines, the speaker in Joanna Hawthorne's marvelous first collection of poems, *How Many is One*, establishes the poet's central motivation for singing her songs.

Ms. Hawthorne's voice is not so much the voice of nostalgia and remembrance, singing the praise of a Golden Age, a past that's always more appealing than the present, but rather, it is a voice of wisdom, speaking directly and unapologetically to the reader about the journey she has taken, one that has brought her reason and understanding, and finally, a strong sense of self won tenaciously through a lifetime of experience.

In this powerful collection, Ms. Hawthorne speaks to us of many things: The force of anger, the loss of innocence, the creation of the world, belief in God, self-dependence, and how living the life she has lived has taught her that being free is the only valid condition for the human being, traveling the long and lone journey, floating down "the river to immortality."

JOANNA HAWTHORNE

On the following pages, basking in her own "age of enlightenment," she enlightens us—anyone fortunate enough to pick up her book and read.

> Mario René Padilla, PHD
> Professor of Creative Writing
> Santa Monica College

INTRODUCTION

Some years ago, I found that I liked to write poetry. Sometimes I was even good at it. But I really didn't know anything about how to do it properly. I didn't know the rules, and everyone knows that you have to know the rules before you can break them, particularly when you're writing. Otherwise, you might not break the rules according to the rules.

So, at the age of seventy, I went back to school. And there I was, me and all the 20-year-olds, seated in a circle and learning how to write poetry. We had to write a new poem each week, and I was totally sure I could not do this. I was totally amazed to find I could. And although I took some liberties here and there with the rules, just like everyone else, nobody minded at all.

The next step, of course, was to put the poems in a book. This scared me all over again, but I got to thinking about the world I live in and all the other people in it, and how sometimes the only thing that binds us all together is our highly varied approaches to spirituality. As I thought about how to build a book of poems around all this, the following came to me.

JOANNA HAWTHORNE

In this life of mine, where I try to deal gracefully with my own shortcomings and disappointments, and to acknowledge without judgment that others do the same, I am increasingly aware of how these inner battles affect the Earth. It is easy to see how our choices and actions impact our environment. It is easy to forget that, if we have the power to impact for ill, we also have the power to impact for good. Remembering to love and care for our world and each other in every moment is possible. I hope that my poems reflect the process in a way that appeals to you.

Joanna Hawthorne

Culver City, California
July 2005

Poetry and hums aren't things that you get, they're things which get you. And all you can do is to go where they can find you.

> —A.A. Milne
> Winnie the Pooh

ME....

Thoughts On Reaching 70
My Stuff
Summer Times
Pemaquid
Steps of Remembrance
Freedom March

Two roads diverged in a wood, and I—
I took the one less traveled by,
And that has made all the difference.

      —Robert Frost
          The Road Not Taken

Do not go where the path may lead;
go instead where there is no path and
leave a trail.

      —Ralph Waldo Emerson

THOUGHTS ON REACHING SEVENTY

Age isn't all it's cracked up to be.
For instance:
I don't <u>feel</u> old, just smarter.
    I don't <u>look</u> old, just larger.
        I don't <u>sound</u> old, just wiser.

By the same token:
I don't <u>feel</u> ill-used, just accepting.
    I don't <u>look</u> stressed out, just busy.
        I don't <u>sound</u> frustrated, just patient.

It's all in the perspective.

For instance:
I don't <u>need</u> men, I enjoy 'em.
    I don't <u>distrust</u> women, I like 'em.
        I don't <u>fear</u> being different, I welcome it.

By the same token:
I don't <u>need</u> companionship, I love solitude.
    I don't <u>distrust</u> fame, I love recognition.
        I don't <u>fear</u> death, I accept the
            inevitability.

BUT!

    I do <u>wish</u> I were fifty again.

MY STUFF

Most people who have desks have one desk.
I have three.

One is a writing desk, left me by my father.
It is small and neat in design.
I do not keep it so.
It holds the usual officey stuff:
    A small gold lamp,
    A letter holder,
    A pencil sharpener,
    A stack of plastic trays full of photos and junk,
    A mug of old pens and pencils,
    Boxes of new and used checks.
It's a mess.

The next is a computer desk, which I bought for myself.
It is large and neat in design.
I do not keep it so.
It holds the usual computery stuff:
    A computer tower, monitor, cable modem,
    A keyboard with a cute little mouse,
    Two speakers, a printer, a scanner,
    A nameplate from working days,

A ceramic '67 Mustang business card holder,
A small bamboo in a vase with a Japanese
    fisherman,
A small puppy with a wrinkled brow lying
    on the monitor,
Computer manuals and supplies,
A typing rack full of papers,
Stacks of papers,
Jars of nuts.
It's a real mess.

Last is my desktop.
That is not a mess!

But the most important of all is the little blue
    book of poetry,
given me by an aunt and uncle in my fourteenth year.
As I leaf through this book, I remember the
    hours of doing so, many years ago.
I greet old friends and places:

The World War I soldier who dreamed of
    "an English heaven,"
A still moment in a snowy wood,
Poor Richard Cory and Miniver Cheevy,
And, most loved, the panther I must not anther.

SUMMER TIMES 1939-1941

One acre of piney woods on a loon-blessed
    lake,
a wood-scented cottage lit by lantern,
heated by fire, watered by pump, two-holer out
    back,
and a path all around laced with poison ivy.

Water lap-lapping the stones at the edge,
water spiders dart-skating now here, now there,
distant hum of a motor boat,
the ssshhh of breeze in the treetops,
and the inescapable zzzzzz of a mosquito.

Girl-child turned into a water rat,
treading the stones and the squish between
    toes,
shivering from delicate brushing of minnows,
moving from cold spot to warm sunspot,
bathing in lake with Ivory soap (it floats).

Going to town by boat then by car,
visiting cousins and uncles and aunts and
    friends,

stocking up on bread, salad greens, cokes,
    apples,
and a big chunk of ice for the icebox,
then lugging it all back by car and boat, to wharf
    and house.

Then night, sent to bed, low voices of adults
    below,
reading The Bobbsey Twins under the covers
    by flashlight,
listening to Tchiakovsky played on the Victrola,
drifting off to the three-toned loon call,
peace, safety, love, contentment, silence
    forever.

The island is still there, remote, unreachable,
    not mine;
I take pictures from the shore but they're not
    enough;
family and cousins, uncles, aunts, friends, now
    gone;
the town the same and different, smaller, but still
    home,
and it's all so far away and only I am left to remember.

HOW MANY IS ONE

PEMAQUID

A curved and open V of blinding white
coasts on drafts thrown upward in sharp blue,
then screeches on its downward plunge.
The knife-drawn line of darker blue horizon
is broken by long dark green humps of islands,
    now here, now there.
Washed in warm sun's brightness and cold
    ocean's spray,
gray rocks of infinite rough variety and shape
crowd, striated, around the tall and sturdy
    tower.

I snuggle into my favorite rock chair with my
    book,
breathing deeply of the pine-tanged air,
and watch the boy, tanned brown as a little
    Indian,
roving over the rocks, searching for treasure,
run and stop, run and stop, checking every little
    pool
left by the farthest reaching drops of great
    waves.
His little gray poodle scampers at his heels,

stopping when he stops, sniffing when he
      inspects a shell.

My father, a grown and future image of the boy,
stands on a flat rock with easel and oils and
      brushes,
gazing out and measuring and touching brush to
      canvas,
meticulously, accurately, lovingly re-creating the
      scene.
From the cottage, I hear my mother send us her
      music
in bits and pieces as she hears it from that inner
      place,
stops and notes it down, then snaps the pencil
      back in her teeth,
and bends over the keys to play the section
      again.

I see from my eye's limit the slight motion of the
      chipmunk
as he darts forward and back, forward and back,
watching for movement, wanting so much the nut
lying in the palm of my hand loose on the rock
      beside me,
then running up and, with a small scratch, taking it,

and dashing back under the trees in terror at his
	bravery.

"Mommy, Mommy, look, Mommy, look!"
The little boy stands high on a rock top,
waving a great flag of seaweed in the air,
the little dog on her hind legs barking in loyal
	praise.
I lift my arm in acknowledgement and the boy
	sits,
happily squeezing the bubbles and chortling at
	each pop.

My eyes are drawn up to the blue, blue, blue.
Please, please, God, don't let me ever forget
	this perfect moment
in this most beautiful place on Earth.

STEPS OF REMEMBRANCE

How well I remember
when I was a little girl
and I was worried or afraid
about a feeling I didn't want to share
and someone my age said, "Me too!"
and I had a new best friend because
I wasn't the only one anymore.

How well I remember
when I was twelve years old
trying to understand being me
and wondering what and why I was
and asking my father what made me "me"
and his patient answer, "It's called ego,"
and I began to feel included.

How well I remember
when I was a wife and mother
believing everyone thought like me
and wanted what I wanted
for the same reasons as I
and learning the hard way
that we are very different from each other.

JOANNA HAWTHORNE

How well I remember
as I grew older and wiser
learning not to expect agreement
and not to judge injustice
and not to depend on others' strengths
and to be responsible for myself
knowing once more I was alone.

Now I will never forget
in my own "age of enlightenment"
that we are both many and one
that our uniqueness is creativity
that our likeness is the source of love
that hatred is denial of these truths
and that we deserve better from one another.

FREEDOM MARCH

I was alone, blessedly alone,
free to sit my life away and read
and smoke and feel guilt,
free to do what I never had time to do before.
Free not to do all those things.
Free.

Then they came and captured me.
They forced me onto the trail,
to walk and walk without respite.
They gave me water and berries.
They gave me pemmican to chew.
They gave me no rest.
They gave me nothing to smoke.

I was afraid.
Not afraid to die, but afraid to hurt.
After a time, I was angry.
How dare they take my freedom?
Then I wept.

I walked and walked, I did not know where.
I walked among the trees, the ferns.
I followed where I was led along that endless trail,
and I wept.

One of them said, "Why do you weep?"
I said, "I weep for what I have never been.
I weep for what I am not now,
and for what I can never be."

And that one said, "What you were, you no longer are.
What you will be, you do not yet know.
What you are now is a trail walker,
breathing pine air,
eating only what you need,
using your substance wisely, to survive,
trusting that the trail will take you home.
No one can do less, or more."

I wiped my tears, and kept walking,
into the next moment, and the next,
free . . .

WE....

He Said, She Said
The Quest
Narcissus Revisited
Resolution
Using the Power
Almost

. . . We must laugh and we must sing,
We are blest by everything,
Everything we look upon is blest.

    —W.B. Yeats
      A Dialogue of Self and Soul

No one can exist as an island.
Relationships are required for success.

    —Jim Great Elk Waters
      View from the Medicine Lodge

HE SAID! SHE SAID!

He said, "I have a project!"
She said, "Tell me about it!"
He thought, "Good! Now I'll have some help."
She thought, "Good! He trusts me."

Sure.
And can't you just imagine what follows?
Imagine how she feels when he orders her to,
"Stand here, lift that, hold it just so, no-no, not <u>that</u>
    way!"
Imagine how he feels when she turns red and hollers,
"Stop it! I'm not your hired help," and stalks off.

She said, "I have a problem."
He said, "Tell me about it."
She thought, "Good. Someone to share with."
He thought, "Good. Something I can solve."

Oh, yeah.
What a jolly mess this gets to be.
Imagine how he feels when she turns red and hollers,
"I didn't ask you to fix it. I just wanted you to listen."

Imagine how she feels when he puts on the poor
    baby face
And whines, "But I thought you wanted my help."

He said, "I need your advice."
She said, "Glad to."
He thought, "Good. This'll get it done faster."
She thought, "Good. Now I can make it right."

Un-hunh.
Oh, boy. We're in for it now.
Imagine how she feels when he turns red and hollers,
"I didn't ask you to change everything!"
Imagine how he feels when she bursts into tears
And sobs, "I was only trying to make it better."

So it is, and so has it always been,
And so will it always be until that glorious day
When we wake up and say, "Hey! I understand you!"

THE QUEST

There once was a mouse from Duluth,
Who set out in search of the Truth.
He took a small rag
To use as a bag,
And a birch twig to clean his front tooth.

He stopped on his way to see Flo
And ask if she wanted to go.
But Flo said, "No way.
What more can I say,
Than that Truth is the one thing I know."

Our mouse shrugged and went further on
To the home of his lifelong friend Don.
But Don only sneezed
And said, "I'm not pleased
At the thought," and he gave a big yawn.

One more stop our hero did make,
At the pad of his big brother Jake,
Who just shook his head
And offered a bed
And promised to bake him a cake.

So there our mouse stood on the road.
His bag had become quite a load.
All alone and rebuffed,
His whiskers he fluffed,
Squared his shoulders and chin, and bestrode.

He trudged on his way all the night,
And when the dawn broke, in the light
He saw his own house
And he cried, "What a mouse,
To go so far when Truth's in plain sight."

The moral of this is quite clear:
To follow a dream you hold dear,
First stop and look 'round
And you'll find that you've found
That the Truth is so near, it's right here!

NARCISSUS REVISITED

Hard, gray, laser eyes, gulping in her creation,
checking, measuring, seeking reassurance
of devotion, obedience, servitude—love?
probably not—why search for the unknown?

Long thin arms crossed tightly over large breasts,
back pressed into the corner of the couch,
long slim legs brought up sideways from the hips,
head of white hair like an old dandelion.

> The creation, told she is beautiful, smart, gifted,
> but never allowed to decide, to know, to try out,
> always dreaming but never able to do great
>   things,
> for fear the cord of possession might be broken.

Tension, pain, two deep downward lines above the
    nose,
dominance and fear dueling for control,
bright, funny, laughing, loving when pleased,
terrifying when crossed.

Hard, gray, laser eyes, gulping in her creation,
she herself formed by distant mother, controlling father,
always searching to fill the screaming void
with obligatory love from the creation.

> The creation, caught in the gray headlights,
> doing whatever is required to be loved,
> beating impotently within for identity,
> knowing there is no reprieve in this life.

RESOLUTION

In search of identity,
    conducted by fear and anger,
    powered by fear and anger,
    paid for with grief, and anger.

Force of anger,
    welling from bottomless root,
    overwhelming intensity,
    energy of life.

Focus of anger:
    Controlling parent,
    waste of years,
    self.

Anguish of loss,
    howling at fortune,
    contempt of cowardice,
    source of hate.

JOANNA HAWTHORNE

Recognition of power:
    Infinity of power,
    destruction by power,
    life through power.

Resolution reveals:
    Anger is desecration;
    force is identity;
    wind of Spirit.

USING THE POWER

Of everything there is, I fear only three—
pain, dismemberment and anger.
(I only fear death if I must suffer.)
No one enjoys hurting,
and no one would want to lose a limb,
but most people do not fear anger.
Strange, because anger is fear.

There are many different kinds of anger.
Dad's anger when Mom spends too much
because he's afraid he can't pay for it.
Mom's anger when Junior runs out in the street
because she's afraid he might be killed.
Gramma's anger when she forgets
because she's afraid of getting old.

There are as many different ways to show anger
as there are people who feel it.
Some totally blow their stacks.
Some smother it until it explodes.
Some eat it until it eats them.
Some use it to terrify, to gain control.
Some die of it, some live by it.

JOANNA HAWTHORNE

The force of anger can move mountains,
and it can save lives.
Uncontrolled anger can cause war,
and it can take lives.
I fear anger because it destroys,
and things said in anger cannot be erased.
Do angry people so want to share their fears?

God must see His creation and weep,
for I think He is afraid for our souls,
and gives vent to righteous anger
hoping that His anger will awaken us.
He knows that the power anger requires
can instead be used to save the world,
for that is the power of love.

ALMOST

Seems to me
it's hard enough
starting out in life with nothing
but DNA and parents
who don't have a clue.

Seems to me
the least God could do
would be to give us
a handicap called
memory!

Sure would be nice
to know who we were before this
and see how far
we've come in striving
to get back to the beginning.

JOANNA HAWTHORNE

So we could say
"now I remember"
as we warp our way
to the next universe and
transformation.

As I see it
if we don't remember
then we have a long hard road to travel
but if we know there's more
then it's all just over the next hill.

And I know
if it seems hard it won't work
but if it feels easy
we're in the flow of the river to
immortality!

S/HE....

First Song
Look At It!
Somebody Goofed
Kritters
The Grand Tour
How Many is One?

There are two ways of spreading the light:
To be the candle or the mirror that reflects it.

—Edith Wharton

From age to age,
Love's word rings forth,
"The truth is true and all is well,
Unconquerable life prevails."

—Martin Exeter
Thus It Is

FIRST SONG

A long, long time ago,
before I, the Earth, was born,
there was music.

It was cosmic waves of vibration,
a great organ, unending,
the universal Word of Creation.

Then I was born,
and my brothers and sisters,
and we were given our tones,
and we began to sing.

Each of us had a tone to sing,
And our singing swept the heavens.
We sang our path through Infinity,
and together we were the choir of Life.

I, the Creator, sang joyously for millennia.
I sang to give birth to water and air,
to bring forth the plants and animals,
and I sang Humanity into being.

JOANNA HAWTHORNE

I, Humankind, sang as I built my shelters;
as I hunted the animals;
as I plowed the rich soil;
and I sang as I gave thanks.

And then, and then, there were two.

You multiplied and peopled the land,
and used my resources to comfort you,
and created new ways to harness me,
so I would give more.

You used me according to your will,
and did not hear me cry out.
You covered my land so I could not breathe,
and slashed and tore at my Eden.

Not so long ago, you could hear the Earth sing.
I do not sing any more.

LOOK AT IT!

Hey, Sad Man!
Hey, Angry Lady!
What is all this?

Stand up!
Get out of your defensive crouch.
Get up off your victim knees.
Shut your ears to doom-sayers.
Close your eyes to graffiti walls.

Wake up!
Can you hear the mockingbird singing everybody's song?
Can you see the flowers pushing through the pavement?
Can you smell the jasmine on a warm night?

What is all this?
The earth pushing forth to bloom yet again.
The ocean still swelling in predictable dance.
The spider still lacing the corner of the room.

The end of the world?
You've got to be kidding!
What we do to others, we do to ourselves.
We get what we give.
What goes around comes around.

I love you.
How can you not love me?

SOMEBODY GOOFED!

Why, oh, why, did I have to be born not knowing?
Why did I have to be taught
every move, every thought?
Why did I not know, remember, all that came before?
Even the flea
is born knowing more than me.
("I", of course; I even had to be taught good grammar.)

Plants don't have to go to school.
They're nobody's fool.
They're programmed by the parent seed.
Genes? We all have 'em.
But genes are only good for the exterior,
and talents, and diseases
like cystic fibrosis
and ragweed sneezes.
(Although some say allergies are signs of low-grade
psychosis.)

Sometimes I wonder, could it be
that once in the dark mists of time
we knew it all in our very bones?
Could we have done something so terrible
that God took back His gift
and we forgot?
Could He have been so discriminatory
that only from us
did He excise the Story?
That doesn't sound like my Friend.
I suspect that, in the end,
We did it to ourselves!

KRITTERS

Curled up in my big blue chair,
Pooh firmly tucked in my right arm,
my left hand scratching Thumper's tummy,
I ponder the sadness.
Why, oh, why can't animals talk?

From early years, I met and loved
Bambi and Dumbo and hippos in pink tutus.
I delighted in mice and spotted dogs,
the adventures of Orlando, the Marmalade Cat,
and, of course, dear Pooh and friends.

There were cats and dogs and turtles and birds
whom I loved and fed and petted and grieved over,
but they couldn't talk!
There were times it seemed they tried
but their talk buttons just didn't work.

And so I am sad at the opportunities missed
to learn what the differences mean,
why dogs are so full of love
and why cats can't give less of a damn,
and to ponder life's mysteries with God's creatures.

JOANNA HAWTHORNE

Sometimes I wonder if I want them to talk
because I almost remember a different time
when Man and the animals spoke without language,
a time when big cats did not attack
and birds did not fly away.

It was a glorious world of love and abundance
where vultures and hyenas did not exist,
and there was no food chain,
a place where Man had nothing to prove
and animals had nothing to fear.

There was great beauty in all kingdoms,
and even the insects were useful,
although I don't think that God created cockroaches,
and I am quite sure He did not inflict upon us
that hungry little wretch, the mosquito!

THE GRAND TOUR

Out the glass door from the den,
down the concrete steps, barefoot,
      past pots of geraniums,
onto the brick walkway, hot, moving fast,
day lilies, juniper, stephanotis to the right,
impatiens and nasturtiums to the left,
then the round white iron table and chairs
      under the wisteria,
still moving fast on hot bricks,
beyond roses and hydrangea
and at last, thank God, cool green grass.

Looking up, up, to the top of tall cyprus,
then turning to small ficus tree,
a garden plot gone to tall weeds
      (no tomatoes this year),
a stunted redwood, juniper hedge,
three liquidamber so high into the wires,
tiny yellow and red flowers beneath,
a fern-lined grotto with St. Francis amid white pebbles,
a great palm with big bunches of white flowers
      and dead brown fronds,
and a small garden of bright colors.

JOANNA HAWTHORNE

A concrete wall painted with an abstract
      of brown earth and green trees,
a tree stump with sundial and more colors,
with little lemon and tangerine and orange trees
      between.
Sharing with our neighbor her jasmine and our
      bougainvillea
intertwined on the wall and over the garage roof.
A small fire pit lined with sand, rimmed with rock,
for solstice and equinox and a full moon.
A small shed to cover garden table and chairs.

Here I see and love a microcosm of nature,
assisted by Man, loved by birds and squirrels,
and offered to Him who made it all.

HOW MANY IS ONE?

Isn't it amazing?

Most people in this world believe in One God,
but they believe in so many different One Gods
that it gets confusing.

People used to believe in many gods,
one for each part of their daily lives,
and it was very confusing.

So eventually most people decided to have One God,
but each group had their own One God,
confusing their neighbors.

Because people tend not to like anyone different,
some try to get others to change to one One God,
to cut down on all this confusion.

Trouble is, they want the One God to be their One
     God
because all other One Gods aren't the same,
causing everybody to be confused.

JOANNA HAWTHORNE

Except in America where each has the right to their
     own One God
so there are probably hundreds, no thousands, of One
     Gods
and confusion is the way of life.

Nobody has discovered that the differences in all the
     One Gods
are really the differences in all the people,
and the One God isn't confused at all.

THE END

BVG